"Unapologetically cosmic in its scope yet always attentive to the tiniest particles of earthling experience, Keegan Lester's all-stops-out debut induces the most meaningful kind of vertigo—one that breaks the spell of habit, sends you reeling, then leaves you radically re-attuned to the world we live in. That world, as Lester presents it, is governed by invisible forces—"we don't choose as much as we think we do in this life," he writes—from the pull of the moon, wind, and molecular biology to the pressures of history, personal memory, actual ghosts, angels, and the will of other people. The sensibility at play in this shouldn't be beautiful... perceives all of the above, and with uncommon acuity. It is akin to that of "the tinkers / & carnie sideshows" who alone can tell "the world's melting"; it feels "the tectonics of things"; it intuits how "unicorns & cowboys are much alive in our DNA" and that "humans are divinity plus movement." Heart-rooted in West Virginia but itinerant in its limbs, this shouldn't be beautiful... is riddled with insight, full of America, made of dazzling cadences, and graced by a "perpetual openness" like that which Emerson ascribes to the Transcendentalist, along with a belief "in inspiration, and in ecstasy." Keegan Lester is just the kind of poet we need right now—and this is inspired, ecstatic poetry." —Timothy Donnelly

this shouldn't be

but it was

so i

beautiful

& it was all i had

drew it

poems
by
keegan lester

Front cover & Interior Designed by Matthew Revert

Cover Photos Copyright © Keegan Lester 2016

Library of Congress Cataloging-in-Publication Data

Lester, Keegan, 1987-

Title: This shouldn't be beautiful but it was & it was all i had so i drew it

  / Keegan Lester.

ISBN 978-0-988-522-15-2

 2016048525

First Edition: February 2017

Slope Editions, created by Ethan Paquin & Christopher Janke in 2001, works toward the goal of presenting readers with a fine and eclectic array of poetry. Each year, we release one to two well-chosen & stylistically diverse softcover, perfect-bound books & chapbooks that defy convention & categorization. Among those who have taken note of our work are Publishers Weekly, Poets & Writers, PN Review, & other publications across the world. Our titles are distributed to the trade by SPD & Baker & Taylor. Slope Editions is part of Slope Publishing Inc., a registered non-profit literary and educational organization with 501(c)(3) status.

for mom & dad & paige

contents

Ghost Note

Coda

Ghost Note

if comets raining overhead. if we turn into a museum for the living before
the big one hits. if language, an improbable opponent to gravity & stars,
came up with new names for gravity & stars, what force could trick a river
north, but the dreams of those who fear sleeping through this version of
the world. if against better judgment we went out at night, run like roman
candles against the wick of sky. if they find us in the riverbank. if our
hearts in our stomachs, a pile of stones, tell them to tie my shoes together.
tell them to throw them over a power line of rusty apricot; silkscreen t-
shirts with our likeness; tell them to inspire bedtime stories in the foreheads
of small children; tell my children to go out at night & sing.

to héloïse d'argenteuil & peter abélard.

to the bones of the pair, moved more than once afterwards,

preserved even through the vicissitudes of french revolution.

to the bones of the pair now presumed to lay
in the well-known tomb in père lachaise cemetery.

by tradition, lovers or singles leave letters at the feet

in tribute to the letters the couple lettered
across oceans of french wheat, in tourist hope

of finding true love. to the angels waiting

with toothy spears around crypt to be called back
home again, not feet away from the other sleeping

lovers no one else will write about in greek, nor latin

nor lit moon sky. to the others like us.

to walking side by side through someone else's graveyard

pondering what will become of us

when summer makes its slight lean & the transfer of remains
more the shaking of two hands, keeping true a promise

written out long before any thought of the anti-plague of honey

locust in the air. to the skin of our lovers, that in time will be
brittle as favorite pages in our favorite books, eventually

mirroring each other. turn saliva into ink.

mouth deliver us to the present, to the people i love today
before becoming a stranger's blanket lit by the lamps

of our heads. to the faint wisps of music, guessing orange

plumage rife from another's time but no less discreet
of the volition of our small lives lived.

grow. to my sister. to the letter i never sent you, it starts with the word *grow*. grow as a tree with no name grows. name yourself. use those roots. use the earth all around you. it's yours. close your eyes. there are some things we're not supposed to look at as we pass: the models, twiggy, strutting by us. look for the monks setting themselves on fire; the mermaids brushing their hair on the jetty; the satellites circling above us. ballerinas are taught to have a point of reference when they spin so as not to grow dizzy— & waiters & waitresses are taught to look toward the horizon so they won't spill & i was taught to watch children run into children in the fall to better understand the strange light we come from. what strikes through a window possesses need. what harpoons is lantern & excess, a button untethered in a pocket for just in case time.

neither of us can be who we are without football. it's true the way a cardinal can't be a cardinal without both wind beneath it & red about it & some nights when i look out into it, into the night & the blacks so close to blue, i can pretend that there's something that tastes better than the pharmaceutical dust i fell for at fifteen, that could make spirals of color of the stars, of the bulbs around our movie theater's marquee, the halos that my grandmother could see too. she called them christmas one evening when she was driving & we knew she needed cataract surgery, but we wasn't gonna say a damned thing. i can feel that christmas now, looking out into it. into just beyond the visitor's grandstand of bleacher. just beyond that. my hand twitching is an indian love call, the slim whitman version & i can hear it over & over in my head, those guitars sliding. it sounds the way i imagine hawaii might sound. but there aren't any indians in hawaii & that was the part of the song most troubling. this is a voice or moon or field of light that can make you forget for a moment the road which you first chose to take. i was like you, down there, beautiful & fatalistic, a body filling time & space. i was once nothing too, nothing chained that couldn't be unchained by stadium light.

the woman i love

is getting married tomorrow.

i slept well last night,

the first time in years.

i woke today new.

i stopped wandering.

i started dating.

i told someone

the clouds look different today.

they said, the *clouds look*

like clouds, & i said

yes, but different clouds.

isn't that great?

i bought myself a fist of roses.

i gave them to strangers & smiled.

some smiled back.

some didn't.

some were falling in love or about to fall in love.

some were being born or about to be born.

we don't choose as much as we think we do in this life.

i built a forest with my mouth & hands,

i have so much time now

that i'm not in love with you.

i grew four inches

& someone told me my eyes look bluer than normal today.

i went to st. john the divine

to look at the phoenix, imported from china.

the bodies that built that phoenix live on

small cots in a chinese factory.

those bodies had always lived there.

one day, a man with long hair approached them
one by one

& said, *can i have your trash,*
you know, the things you consider sacred,

to make this thing for others?
i tried not to fall back in love,

but everyone was doing it.
everyone was someone else too,

their better self, while they were doing it.
it's a scary thing, all this introspection.

i was once at a county fair in indiana.
someone there bragged

this was the second largest county fair in the country.
they were feeling safe & proud

eating their fried kool-aid,
playing name the dead deep fried animal

we just ate game

& had no idea that my county fair is the largest in the country.

they would sleep easy that night

not knowing

my ferris wheel can be seen from space,

& whatever flew above us knew we existed

as a cog in this great lit up machinery

of hands notching other hands

to make lips move,

to make night fall into its place,

to make the sun come up the next morning.

i wasn't gonna say a goddamned thing either

because love too is like a county fair,

in that it's at its best in the dark,

next to someone you just met.

deer electric in the air will live another day
is the one thing we count on

to change. we count on them to grow wings
& to cocoon. put these hills on

my shoulders. i know it takes more to be born
again, than the hills i've placed

myself. my father, when he arrives, will have his
cardboard box filled with black walnuts

in the passenger seat. i've never known what he does with them.
i've never asked. he will try to pull the sheets over

someone's eyelids. he will try & try
& try. he will say: *what's the thing on the side of the old*

mashuley house. the leaves haven't quite turned yet.
it will take the internet to

convince him the word for the shape painted
is f hole, to convince him

if a house had a rib this is the place where cartilage
stretches taut: my grandma's whispering

beneath her breath: *it's about to pour the rain*
not a cloud in the sky.

are we all not a little wounded? had you broke
icarus's wings with your own hands,

he would have whined. had you broke icarus's wings
with your own hands,

his life would have been spared. that's why there's no mother
in that story. these are the choices

determining what we shrub into later on. are you capable of
breaking another's wings by yourself?

a blue wind sent me. *you have penguin wings*, i was told.
was told there are things i can do

with these penguin wings that will save all lives

but my own. these are the hills i learned to speak in.

this the neighborhood splitting my lip

blue, that never apologized, has everything to show for it.

my liver is full on this neighborhood,

its tiny glass castles & its white flag dogwoods that die & die &

die in late spring's frost. my liver is waiting

on a mouth of mechanical light.

my liver is waiting on a mouth & the person with

the stones required to sink it.

to my mother painting hummingbirds: the feeding & caring for something else is the art part in all of this. to learning how light changes relationships. as a child it's easy to think people & love are both infinite things. to algebra, geometry & geographic information systems. to what i wrote years ago when we were still everything we made & everything we made a gift for someone else. to these things we are: little more than what we bring to our ear. to the bells st. francis introduced to christianity, borrowing from islam a call to worship: first the smaller ones, then the larger ones. to the morning i swore i could hear your heartbeat laying in bed next to you, my ear in the nook between your neck & chest. if there is a book to prove me wrong about the factual possibility of the location of that pulse, it exists because the writer has never been in love thousands of miles from home. to the book & the writer of the book who's never been in love thousands of miles from home. to the low hanging fog strangling the lights around portland, blinking morse code into the clouds. to the games clouds play when people are looking.

with all the things we ask children to perform
in war, it's no wonder war's popularity.
somewhere else, we're done dancing. we're
picking our clothes up off your living room floor
for the second time today. one day, i'll listen
as you sing, as you avoid cutting your knees
with a razor blade in a tub with talons on its feet.
one day i'll tell you about the picture show
at the brooklyn waterfront, where summer
had forgotten how to be summer & i shared
a stranger's apple juice spiked with vodka &
missed my flight the next day. that's the reason
i was late & we didn't touch cheeks that night.
this is the morning i listen for the birds outside to
speak in a language as much theirs as it is ours,
that can leave us just as easily. this is the morning,
very much like the moment before the moment
happens— where everything's still
somewhat unexplainable. if i had a time machine,
i'd use it. i'm no superman, but you already knew

that. the radio in the corner of this place is talking
about the piles of bodies piled atop other bodies
in trenches from a country whose dirt our neighbor
collects in 32 ounce wide mouth jars in his garage,
labeled with calligraphy sharpie on duct tape.
if i had a time machine, it would be black with ink.
it would run on the power from the flux capacitor
in the cartilage between my ribs, where i listen
better to all the strings attached to other theories
about strings attached to christmas lights, where for better
or mostly worse, something blooms out that hasn't been
written yet. i've done the division of maps & sleep
over time, forgetting to carry the zero, where
everything invisible is still waiting.

to the supermarket: a dash of color, then the fluorescent feeling more like an explosion.

to the song: the impulse to reach out turning to a need: to see not only with eyes.

to new martinsville: lead us both somewhere else.

to your father pulling his hunting knife on me.

to the polaroid of you in seattle, now with the other polaroids: a deck of dim lit faces.

to the space needle, to the sound & to the wakes of boats.

to the yellow beach pail filled with sea glass.

to the child chasing seagulls.

to the sun burning the fog on the fringes.

to ben gibbard, david bazan & jenny lewis.

to the daisies in belfast that summer: i'll never forget, they smelled just like the daisies in west virginia.

(if you want them, take them. if you sit long enough with them, they may teach you to dance).

to the night my father told a bartender *belfast is the reason my son stopped attending church.*

to the true reason i stopped attending church.

to the sunday mornings you taught me to sleep in.

you said *god is in everything,*

you said *god is most especially in learning to cook my coffee up right.*

there was once the heavens & the oceans. there was once the chicken & the egg,

there was once the atom & the eve & then gunfire. & then there were the oceans

& beaches, adams & eves, chickens & eggs, human life & the halting of human life.

there was once two owls in a sugar maple, field mice below & an afternoon settling

behind the mountains, throats cut by the monongahela river, copper blood spilling

from them. no suture could close this thing, & night soon hid it momentarily.

in the morning the field mice disappeared behind the sleight of hand of the crouching

owls & the riverbed's copper veins showed & while beautiful, it was easy

to see the earth would not have the stomach for more of this business & so sold its shares

& retired to an undisclosed island hiding elvis, tupac & richie valens. when they find us,

we will all be trilobites. our hearts & hands & eyes, all small star critters etched

into some rock. the rocks will outlast us & anything we had to say about us. & we

the mason jars of lightning bugs in the dark. & we, what is swallowed by light.

there was once a projector playing back home movies of what we are actually like

in real life but was lost in a tragic cinema house fire. now none of us have to look

at each other. words mean almost anything i want them to mean. *we too are*

the protagonists, we are small gods, the owls hwooo into the night, no matter how

silent the field mice remain.

rather than fearing the repercussion of

together, we could share all the ghosts

we've danced with. had i known more

of the independent variables, what postcards

were invented for: dear mother, no one sees

the glaciers trickle into ocean the way

i dream of them at night. i dream

a hole & a fist. i dream sea floor opening

& opening & time is the arms of the atlantic.

the arms of the atlantic separating two

continents, for now. the math works out

like that. the math confirmed: a forest

petrified, would stay petrified even if

no one is around to hear its colors.

its colors tell the stories of our stories

now, even if no one is around to hear them.

its colors telling the stories because facts

don't paint pictures. in o'hare i walk beneath

the terminal, the magic dwindled, once a

passage: it's easier to see our faces in the marble

now that we know we're average. there are

no special snowflakes. we've become what

we've watched from afar. we've become

the photos we orchestrate into meaning.

in the next new life we are moving toward

another new life, but someone asks that we

stay like this. you said *it reminds me of the*

neon rain at a christmas party years ago,

a bottle of grey goose in passing, *when i was*

young. how brief people in my life would

stay i was never warned when i was young.

they came & left an atlas unfinished that every

now & then i glance at to better understand the shoulder

 of highway i've pulled off, onto: the blacktop

glistening in oklahoma: chewing sunflower seeds

at night, breaking husk with molar, removing husk

with tongue, spit. then repeat. break husk, tongue,

spit. repeat, in a region where all that's left are ghosts

dancing for other ghosts, for you & me, for the

burnt out song we used to sing.

to all of this which does not just seem, but is extraordinary.

to a time when extraordinary was a thief machine.

to the thief machine & the small hands needed to operate that machine.

to the hands of children that adults go to when they lose something.

to the unbroken thinking of children.

to the something foreign, the feral, to the different ways light breaks

against the faces my mother catalogues: always growing, fig not far from the branch.

when you asked do you have to be sad to write poetry & i said no, but i have to have learned something

i was watching the direction your knees were pointing. when i was young, it was the act of praying.

i'm trying to thank you. i'm waiting on a text message. i'm trying to figure out what the other

three signs were, walking balmy lanterned morgantown bridges. it looks more west virginia here tonight

than ever. i had to relearn everything after i stopped drinking. i've reclaimed verbs for want & confusion.

you drove an hour back from wheeling, the day we met. later on the phone you said it was because

you were horny, but i like to think teen movies & romance. i like to think everything rustling in the bushes

is a ghost, fox or beer can. i haven't told you yet but i don't have tattoos because i hate

what needles are capable of. you kissed me & my brain rewired into sliced pears, grainy, looking

for what exists not what could & still i have some relearning to do. i'm not wondering what love is

or knowing but thinking i want to bake chocolate coconut brownies with you. have you ever held a baby duck

in your hands? you probably shouldn't, but one time i did, & it was nothing like holding a child.

for the first time i had a sense of my own mortality, a ring of ducks surrounding my body, but

they were geese because geese are more imposing. & there is nothing sad about changing a word

to make something seem closer in a poem to the cicadas that were never as cicada electric as i

remember them to have been, as electric as the electric blue i conjure every now & then when i come

across your name.

brca1 is a human tumor suppressor gene, which produces a protein called breast cancer type one. it once stood for berkeley, california, where perhaps two lovers in stiff vanilla pressed lab coats, living months on chinese take-out & bad cafeteria food, went from lab to bedroom to lab until they discovered what this translated. one must have turned to the other like the driftwood lapping against the shore forty miles away, needing something to land upon after having been lost at sea too long, & said: *look at the variation, at the movement.*

to when there are no cameras left to translate the quiet.

to when i think in the backyard: you'll never be manhattan.

to the bark winter peeled back, turning tree trunk into the faces

of the imaginary forepeople helping me found this place. &

like rushmore we make postcards to help preserve their memory

during the summer months. & like rushmore, the faces in the trees

look smaller in real life. to everything i've ever loved for overlooking

the sovereignty of your life without me. for not seeing you were

too big for the stadium pools they kept you in after the show. we are all

created equal parts stardust & i gathered with the rest each fall to watch

the strongest collide into each other in front of stadiums & someone

calls this the italian renaissance, medieval, the end of civilization: beauty

finds such crush inside beauty. to what was above us, had always been

above us & what was around us now apparent only in its indifference

to what we once thought. to this town: a blistered & broken mouth—i admit

i was high when i first noticed the tectonics of things, their movements—

the oxiheads on the staircase now younger than me. & these our mouths.

& these our stars to share.

dear mother, the first christmas that did not feel like christmas, on christmas day i was sitting in an ihop

listening to my uncle make fun of people just like my uncle & home stopped being home & i took a bus

back to new york city. when i came out the holland tunnel all the buildings surrounding me were mine,

& the stomach of that city was mine, my home, & i stepped off that bus & right back into the streets

& then into a building where i exist as one of the millions of windows my neighbors will encounter

in their lifetime

& these mountains i go to, i go to

because the ones i wanted to be

born in are not mine. & what is

not mine does not leave me.

to the four women reading me my tarot

this month. you should be

looking for the girl that will

change you, they all said. & in the morning i notice

frost in the windowsill

of a room i've never been in before. to the slow

eyed sara bareilles song

my captor plays. to the girl,

holding the kind of secrets of perched owls.

too sick to go

home, i think of her. i think distant planet. i think the tilt

of audrey hepburn's head.

the tilt when her character is pretending

to be confused, not when audrey

herself is acting out

real confusion. there's a difference.

it's slight but real. tonight has the eyes

of thawed lakes. words are no good

for this. i break

my hands on my eyes.

i break my ears on a mouth. the ghosts all around me

do their dance. they lift

mountains that are not mine to hold

from me. they lift

mountains that are not theirs

to lift, & when i see you again, mother,

i'll tell you how all this started,

because when stars cease to be stars

what we see is stars

& what we call them is stars.

the race ends under caution.

everything said saturday night sounds didactic

sunday morning, so won't you just

hold my hand? let's celebrate

the game of connect four, the plastic discs

chuting, their plastic clunk

landing on top of one another.

the sound is so satisfying

i think we could become clams,

pearls replacing our hearts,

always a bus leaving chinatown

toward where the dead will not follow us.

make me malleable & tough & the world a phantom of clouds,

picasso. picasso, are you outdated?

who is the person in charge of that these days?

you know, looking at something,
shifting its shape until its outsides more closely resemble

its insides. i created a dance last night

called the elephant trunk. absolutely
none of the kids are doing it, yet.

i checked dance halls,

fire escapes & seedy places housing romantic charm
(our local seven-eleven bathroom)

& no, no one was doing it. i'm sick of that

boring poetry that has fifty ways
to describe death, love & de-leafed trees.

there are things we can do

with our arms & legs that will make us look
like smaller people.

things we can rename ourselves

based on the expressions of our face
when we almost get to where we are going.

there are so many things
i was unsure of

until i went looking.

to the plains of musashi.

to the teachers living for the headlines
of the national enquirer.

to the moon once silver,

but blackened by age,
worn out, you say. it's sad, you say,

face pressing glass

as close as security will let you
to the fan of grass chuting,

as close as security will let your face

press against the moon
slipping, the crane necks tucked

for flight. to as close as they will let you

press your face to the bowl of peaches,

placed there for longevity.

to the hairs i find on my clothes

when you're gone,

the apparition of you

a bruise to skin, saying: notice me.

so i did. i started writing this

in the metropolitan museum,

as your neck bent

to touch your nose to the worn out japanese moon.

i started writing this to appease your hairs

& the apparition of you,

then to conjure that which comes & goes

in white ball gowns.

to the nights your ghost waits

for me on the roof, to sing our song

together, fisting guardrail, our neck

craning as we make our reach for moon,
first with our noses

then tongue, an oyster membrane,
shell, vodka & tomato paste. i show you

how my father taught me

what to do with oysters.
to my father & his stories

dreaming on & on, shucking

the flesh of oyster in balboa,
a little more horseradish on the next

he'd say, & the moon over the bay,

the bay beneath its pillow,
we all lie where we stand, dead prisoners

my grandmother says meaning
to the cacophony of moonlit rooms

we are shackled.

to her stack of love letters

in the bottom drawer of her armoire
we go to when she forgets who she is.

we talk of the coming & going of our apparitions,

together. we count one, two, three, four.
we're anywhere our sleep has thought

or seen to make room for us.

i don't want to be saved
by my lover, my lover says to me

with her eyes closed
on a park bench,

& the al pastor is a little too chewy

& our stomachs turn us into less sexy versions of ourselves
in our heads, but we are old now anyways.

sexy is relative. we are like two thirteen-year-olds at a dance on opposite sides of the room,
waiting to make a move & our eyes meet during that country grammar song

& nelly's syntax makes us believe
 in what entire flocks of seagulls can be capable of,

miles from a beach.

every time a person takes a selfie,
a piece of them dies.

a little, a sacrifice to the selfie gods,

she says. *grow a beard & close your eyes when you kiss me,*
she says, with her eyes closed.

i don't want the fireworks

in the street to be terrifying, but they are
& i know i'd make a terrible soldier, every time i look in the mirror

i say. & i know i shouldn't be

telling you all this here
but i don't want to be saved by my lover either. i want

pomegranates & dark chocolate,
the kind of mountains mouths make

when at rest

at the kitchen table
tomorrow morning.

in florida

the mangroves hide egrets & manatees & fish
& budweiser cans too

she says to me,
as if they are all the same thing.

& maybe she's right.

florida is the last place in this country
where it's still legal,

if you're in a pinch,
to bury what you value in a chest deep inside the earth

for others to find later on

& *in florida it's still legal*
to have sex on high school football fields

& smoke in bowling alleys, she says.

i look at her. &
it's alright. i mean, i'm not perfect either.

there are entire bodies of water
people call ocean,

& ocean is the name

for both the space we cannot fathom seeing

& the surface

& i want to be your gremlin fish

a light above my head,

searching in the black, black water, i say.

it begins as it always begins, i couldn't help from thinking

hundreds of years after us, after this country of the explorers

wandering through overgrown forest or jungle or the fringes

of post-nuclear apocalypse or what have you, stumbling

upon these ancient football stadiums. we will have made the ghosts

of greece & rome blush at what they thought they could accomplish

with their hands. we, our ghosts, will be equal to their ghosts.

& come autumn when there's quiet away from the traffic noises,

i will stand very still & listen. the dark will be arcing above then

& one will detect wisps of sibilant lisp & call notes, the voices

of migrant ghosts keeping in touch. their calls scattered through.

without wave of feeling—a lonely distance of small lives directed

by our choosing of denial, a mendacity. a wonder at the sure instinct,

route & direction that so far has baffled efforts to explain it.

the night will be alive then, with the calls of these migrant ghosts.

it begins with something. it begins with something so large,

america relearns to imagine again. it begins with a creation story

where entire flocks of ghosts, angels & holy ghosts molded from clay

into being overnight, after the ball hung to sky the first time

& our knees grew wobbly from looking & that spiral was beautiful,

was a siren with grit & teeth. it was a sirens's sweet

hook, suspending flesh for reach. it begins when he turns fifteen,

understanding the sad the siren must endure. he thinks

just as he cannot sleep with her, she cannot sleep with him.

this made him different from the others, both player & spectator.

this keeps him looking up at night. the lightposts keep him. the

obstacles are all still there, even with nothing chasing.

it begins with a brazen scar threading sky, afternoon setting,

night setting to morning & he's too tall to hide. just because

his body is capable doesn't mean it has to or that he necessarily should,

or to be loved by a stranger for his body is the same as being loved. it

begins with you, injured boy. ambulance bulleting toward hospital.

in the hospital three nurses enter a room with white walls, floral trim

slicing the mid-section of wall into two fields. nurses cut jersey

with scissors methodically from your body like lichen from

arctic tundra, as something that's endured, as something to

save. nurses cut helmet from your head with a small electric saw. remove shoulder

pads with the diligence one uses when removing marrow

from bone, before untying your shoes, right first & then left &

placing them in a neat pile next to the door. they follow

all the protocols for cutting you down & turning you human again.

& what good is it to be human, like us? in america

there are protocols in matters like this. it begins at seventeen. it begins

precious human body & your mother & father who don't drink coffee

at this hour, often commenting on it to be polite at dinner parties, drinking coffee in the waiting room. the nurses prep you

for surgery as the game returns to play. doubt

in the crowd's conversation is also protocol, as is yelling

of a new boy's name, & it's when they hear the echo

of themselves throughout the stadium they galvanize. they forget

anything that is not themselves. they cross themselves,

they fill with something, with something like fourth of july sparklers

or christmas or halloween costumes, a surprise kiss at the office party

or the vacation they save up all year to make themselves sick

on karaoke in a foreign country where everyone native speaks english too,

but speaks an english not recognizable to their english at all.

what only moments ago sounded borrowed begins to leave the diaphragm

like home. it begins to sound royal blue & white again. it begins

again when a boy is asked to fill the unfillable void. it begins

with a man whispering into that boy's ear: *you're captain of the unsinkable.*

it begins with a boy's pass thrown blindly into coverage. it begins

with an audible into & from nothing. the boy will not notice

the defensive ends cheating up. it begins later that night, the boy sitting

on his porch looking at a moon that feels like it's frowning.

& the moon is frowning, & somewhere in the distance, beneath

the frowning moon a meadowlark barks out what sounds more like a cadence

than a warning. it begins after the lights turned out & the dairy

queen closed last friday night when you said: *nothing about this feels seventeen.*

this is when you go back to being children again

& it turns early saturday morning & we see the stars against west texas sky

because no lights are on, nowhere. *we need* the girl whispers

in the backseat of an ocean blue ford, glittering beneath the moon. this ford

is the only thing here glittering or ocean.

this ford might as well be a spaceship. & it begins in the movie version

where she escapes that small town & begins again in the book version where she doesn't

& in the television version it's unclear. after your early morning whispering

i realize the only drama that still exists is what has not been written out,

which is why we love football & west texas where nothing is

written, & it begins when stretches of highway feel roman, connecting fields

of mechanical horse oil drums & fields of sand & fields of cattle

to fields of grass & fields of night which meets vision miles & miles

long & wide. & that vision is also an ocean, deep & treacherous, an ocean

in the old days sense, when the world was still flat & you could see the next continent

because there was no curvature of the earth yet capable of dissuading

that ocean, & yet, people got lost in their tiny boats all the time. it begins

because my books are more intimate than my pillow, & all the subway stops blur

into west texas towns, where everyone closes their eyes to what kills the town,

puts everything into closing their eyes so that when they open

stained cardinals can fly from them, if only for a couple hours on a friday night.

it begins because kids playing are the only magic in that town.

those kids are a well of magic & bird, & only a well of magic bird can get a town to sleep.

it begins if i forget the language, i forget a part of me & you said keegan

what am i gonna do now, i can't do nothing but play football

& the hole inside my head is growing. it's not true what they say about hearts, you know.

what they don't tell you is we are made of the circuitry of our brains,

the lights a carnival, a carousel with an infinite journey that keeps turning. what they don't tell you

is that as the bulbs go out, the animals inside that carousel grow feral,

& then double-cross the machinery. & it can never cease to move, because if the machine stops

the sun comes up plain as day & you see everything you are,

because you are nothing. take note, it's always easy to see what you are

when you are nothing or dead. so even as the bulbs go out & because we are a beautiful

& an expansive machinery, a machinery that can't stop, there's no way to replace those bulbs.

what they don't tell you is our hearts got nothing to do with nothing.

they're just the fists in our chests that clench & unclench. it begins the night we didn't win state,

she pulled me close, but i was in no mood to fuck & with only fake pearls on, she said

darling, it was just a game & i knew it was but

just can be deceiving too, as eyes & what we take eyes to mean. who's to say

whether your pearls are plastic or dove i said the night we met

after thinking i'd met everyone there was to meet in town. & it felt the way

someone once told me chewing on toothpicks makes me look like a hick,

as i chewed on a toothpick, after buying that girl dinner. i relished it, because if i didn't

it would swallow me. it begins with one building kindness with their eyes, before learning

to use them for destruction. it begins because the necklace that i thought was pearl,

the night on a fire escape where we danced because dancing is all drunk people know

how to do, was not pearl. & she liked that i didn't know the difference

& she liked that i couldn't help but think hundreds of years after us, after this country

of the explorers that would be looking for treasure, the stadiums here they would instead stumble upon, seeing what i see now,

as they wander through our god particles.

my mother is sick & cannot leave her bed most days.

i am of my mother & therefore i am sick too.

i am of my mother & so i race to find a cure for us.

i leave that house & walk away from the dim lit faces

of the mumbling televisions. *my mother is sick & therefore i am sick too*

i tell the woman i sleep with. i leave that house

spanish moss hangs from a tree growing in brooklyn

& it's a terminal thing i share with my mother.

you are so much like her my father shakes his head

side to side in a bar, *i always feared you would be*

& paige, that way he says, after telling him the prognosis.

i ate my hands to keep from touching myself.

i gave my things away, only to come back to bed surrounded

by the things i'd given away. *you haven't been right*

for some time my friend says, while she

dips her hands between my thighs— thinking maccabee,

thinking oil, —& other miracles in the wrong language.
my mother is sick & i am of her & therefore i am sick

too, i say. what surrounds us are not ghosts
but one another. if i could claw my eyes out to keep from seeing

i would, but i ate my hands & talons
just last week, in an attempt to cure this thing—

would you be a dear & take them from me?
you would still be able to feel the gravity of the earth

my friend says. *you'd still feel the moon tugging the oceans.*
i know, i know, but i've got to try something i say.

if i could get milkweed or whatever you want
to grow from the holes in my face, if i'd been better

at folding paper cranes, pronouncing dubious words
in their native french, at least one of us

would have had a chance to leave here with something
we wanted.

both our language & the air carrying our language

were birds &
more birds.

our mouths vanished.

i had to relearn to touch you in the room where we created art,
the art that could no longer be heard in the art.

i want to thank catholic school for being the bully on the playground
& the teacher that saved me from the bully.

you said: *we all need*
to work on growing

our own crown of teeth.

you'd survived the war,
i read on the television,

from learning to dance.

from your kitchen's linoleum floor

that you'd gotten good at picking your body up from.

if you can imagine from

meaning: everything your hands touch:

the perennials that no longer

weed those hands

beneath motel sheets in pittsburgh.

i read you your from

as place

as in where deer tracks fawn,

but also a prism

       though which light enters

you, which leaves you no longer just human.

& the bend of sycamores

on the bus ride back to new york city,

a levy of our secret.

& for better or worse, birds

flew from us

as a metaphor for anything with the potential to break

us new.

you said tilt your head like this.

you said speak to me

with your talons.

i read you your yellow parchment skin, burnt at the edges, where they buried your human

(or what was left of your human).

i read that after the war you said not every soldier was a hero. the woman holding the microphone

did not realize you meant yourself.

& no longer just a human, you've taken to talking to the hung up sun. after the war, i read &

reread on the television, people took until the sun

exploded & the earth grew cold. the trees turned to lean-to twigs propping up sky, then turning

into our hands reaching.

*

night left us waiting for the breeze

strong enough to task us
with starting over again,

should we luck the starry sky ceiling into caving

during the night. there's so much hope
we'll feel safe from the dark again

with all the other small animals

when morning rises.
we will continue

to live like this until evolution

teaches the other small animals

that though small & fuzzy
they were not meant to be squeezed by us.

they are not our dreamcatchers,

our therapists

or diaries.

we are a thing to be feared.

& when we run out

of small fuzzy animals

on the black market

to squeeze,

because they only go out at night,

which we will fear

with post-apocalyptic revelry,

we will stuff

our books

& learn to go to them for safety.

*

on the television, i've seen our death
play out on the local news,

john beard looking stoic as ever,
his mustache of power

making the terrible news of our demise
feel a little more tolerable.

the image flashing on the screen behind him
looks like cherry blossom season

to a people who had never seen cherry blossom season.

it looks like all the things we can't imagine
knowing how to fear yet,

because no one taught us to fear correctly.

it looks like the hands of small children,
their magnifying glasses melting figurines

of their strangers & their friends.

that soon pears would

        taste like pears again,

a new country to sleep in

was all we could hope for.

we considered

we were both dying.

a drape pretending in a window

        across broadway. he heard ghosts speaking

in passing footsteps. i watched him

smoke cigarettes to ash,

the trees shiver,

the marble buildings straight. i peeled

clementines.

i ate each crescent.

what started as a whisper

filled the trees in place of their pine

needles.

another person's heart wasn't his. in his poem i watch

two girls make their way

        past

the three of us

& my hands weren't mine.

she sings because she thinks no one can hear her.

he could not stop hearing her.

the amount of honey

produced in the life of a honeybee made him

heartsick too. he was a native of nowhere.

if it were to rain, it would have been an excuse

        to go dancing.

he used the word nude

because it was correct.

he knew a rumor was there, what else
would fit

the space?

he named the thing
a girl's hands

were doing: finching.

that, that itself is a kind of entropy,
he knew only how to unfold maps.

he called her songs:
neurosis

of the pulmonary artery. he knew
a heart removed

from a brain

tries to pump
before dying, but a brain

removed from the heart burns

out quiet like a distant constellation.

he knew by some accounts
          native americans mistook the sails of genocidal explorers
for clouds.

he knew aboutness the primitive

language for doing, the sky to be inky
& the moon to be 250,000 miles away.

the younger poet knew

how the curtains moved
in her window

when no one was there to move them.

i wrote a love poem

to amanpour & it started:

once when walking

behind my uncle's cul-de-sac

through a handful of suffocating

woods, i discovered a hole

in the ground & i put

my fist in it.

i didn't know that i

didn't know i shouldn't have,

until years later. needless to say,

i'm still not afraid of snakes,

though i'd feel better

about camping if grizzly bears

stopped shitting in the river.

i'd feel less alone waking

up each morning if the newspaper

stopped pretending to be deaf

& we had a real conversation

over coffee. i'd like to

blame my depth perception

more often for getting caught

amidst jewelry heists.

i'd probably have done right

more often if i'd been

more color blind &

everything was black & white.

i'd pay more attention

if newscasters stopped

being so attractive.

i'd stop falling in love so easy,

if it wasn't so easy to do.

i don't always think we should

leave music up to the professionals,

unless that professional

is ray charles. i'd stop riding the bus

if the old vietnamese women

would stop gossiping.

my father called me downstairs last night

to watch a speech on the television.

he said, i'm so afraid

for our future. & i believed him.

it was the first time he'd been afraid

of anything in front of me.

i'd be more afraid of their silence

i told him. i'd be more afraid

of their sticks & stones,

their words won't eat your atoms

to my father confiding in me. to the icebergs we've become, the bits of ourselves making up the ocean where we touch everything, & everything is made of us, & to the ship crashing into us each day, only seeing the small that makes itself visible. to a life that passed us by. to relearning together. to the slow sad his feet make, turning up the stairs each night. to the extinguished television. to the castle he built. to the walls he built around that castle. to the sound of his '93 astro van's engine turning over, the first sound i would recognize as his & only his. to his story that begins & begins & begins *when i was about your age on the banks of the seine, with a couple jugs of wine & this girl…* & it begins again later with another of the pinned back european rivers my father dreams of.

1940s berlin in a movie theater, where two strangers touch each other & the hair raises on his arm, & they blame it on the wind, & they can't tell from that vantage point, but the moonlight is just right.

i thought i saw you again, this time in
cambridge. i kept double taking all night
over my shoulder & the malls of america
have grown empty windows now. i had to
walk through the mall to get to the prudential
& snow made a bed of the city. there wasn't
anything else to do. people started walking
on water, & skipping acorns across the icy
topographical veins. i saw a lighthouse
from fifty floors up. i saw it blink back.
it was the first time i ever saw a real lighthouse
blink. the airplanes were more seagulls
air beneath wing, making their slow
descent all around us. everyone was
either on their way or about to be. it had been
years since i was here, & i realize, now, we are
supposed to have learned what we have not.
my friend says *you should come back*
in the summer or spring, but what's the point?
what is boston without a brutal fugue of wind
& ice & brick. my friend told me a story

last night. i thought only of eleni's father

paraphrasing for me in the kitchen before i left,

we all should be weary of poets who dream to be sailors

rehearsing the way he'd do it when in the hospital,

looking his friend in the eye, the terrible proliferation

of equipment all around them & i could almost hear

the whales that swim our dreams & i could almost

understand what they were trying to tell me.

nothing seems impossible after it's already happened,

& still people will. & still people will. we need

people in our lives who will what we won't.

we need the snow to help us see what we can't.

& if you see me double take over my shoulder,

it's only because i thought i'd seen a ghost or beacon

or you across the room.

while i was out getting drunk night after night, there were entire collectives of people searching for lions. lions with thorns in their paws. as these sightings became more & more rare some resorted to placing thorns nearby, hoping to plant seeds in the minds of these majestic & furious beasts until one night black stopped being black, until even the petals on stems people went to for guidance were cloaks placed by someone else: *she loves me, she loves me not*, she a brazen erupting star, she the sacrifice to appease something that was made up. we were asked to wash the priests' hands. to wait until we could see images in the heads of match flame. no greater enemy exists than the self-conceit of our own wisdom. i was left completely unequipped for what to push up against walls, over desks, through black holes. i was left completely unequipped for the becoming part, for the end, for the fingertips of the cosmos. the one thing i know is real is that my grandmother used to steal coal from her father to warm her school house. that was her job: steal coal, so other children could learn to read. when you think of west virginia, think of her.

to the egrets & wasps. to 2052 lincoln park west.
to the couch pretending snow, you sleep: wind
displacing your body shape. you like to sleep
listening. to who thought to make this the measuring
stick. the measuring stick makes us pine for the duplicity
of our lives lived versus lives shown, wind between
two buildings squeezing snow, dreamy into the park
& then lake & running as if twenty-year-olds onto a
football field, the slate clean of stars. run toward
whatever exists on. run toward the other side of the body
of water, far from the horned buildings & the stadium
power: the amalgamation of 70,000 people's magic
realism on the television set. run far from the blinking eye-
lids & storefronts. you're an argyle wire fence
curled up at the bottom. you let impossible sneak in.
your sleep is a manifest destiny outward, as the gulf
of mexico is also someone else's sleep, further someone's
wake, far from each twinkle, twinkle, little superfluous
shadow growing across the map of your face.

humans are divinity plus movement plus bed sheets & a car driving away from town against night
& a red planet in the northern lake of black hemisphere & the shots scattering the trees. the birds
in the trees scattering too. no one thought to notice what kind of birds they were because there wasn't time
to name birds. morning noosing sky above the motel two humans met at the night before who did not draw
back the blinds. each other's body out & like teenagers again, only more knowing & less fragile in their
breaking of each other's body, meaning it's now time. the shot could have come from anywhere in memphis.
one says to the other. the other says: the light means it's time. morning is both time & place. they will
have to wait another eleven hours until stars & planets can piece this thing together. & voices outside
the room are keeping secrets too, about fragility. the voices outside the room are teaching their own
methods for breaking. & breaking means we. & we must begin looking again means human.

i like it when you grab me by the neck & bite me
to prove facts.

i feel i have something worth recollecting
later on like world war one,

when you could pick any country you wanted to fight for, & just fight for it,
learning to hate a stranger's foreign words

enough to think them similar to a peach,
both beautiful & hairy

a sunset leading to a stomach full of bayonet,
making that stomach bloom & burst &

cringe, an orchid in its own field

when later you could go into town at night for whiskey & cinema,
maybe a blowie in an alleyway depending

on which country you chose to fight for. i was drunk when someone tried to explain diplomacy to me:

if country a wants country b, then country a calculates the resource expenditures
it would take to gain country b, versus the total sum of resources gained.

no one at this wedding thought let's just leave country b alone.
let's just stick to hunting people for sport & the hustle,

except me, but i was twelve & algebra confusing.
but maybe that's a lie.

i can remember telling someone in the nineties
joining the marines seemed like a good idea.

i didn't know there were still wars left to be fought
& where else to begin but with foxes:

foxholes just make war seem sexier
even though the evidence leans toward

a planet that's lost its axis.

after the war against bougainvillea,

each weekend my childhood driveway's

concrete could not prevent petal nor thorn

from hand. after i was west again,

cherry blossoms bloomed. after a

hummingbird crashing into my mother's window it

kisses concrete before passing

on. & after that, i'm older now,

it's my job to carry the dead before it

upsets the others. after picking its body up

in a napkin, the weightlessness forces me

to wander a blue sky, a dim lit sky, a red

sky, a road that knows no invisible

geographic border, a crustacean on one end

& yucca on the other. after i wonder,

i'm sorry for missing the cherry blossoms bloom

this year only because it was a thing we do

together. though, had i missed this, how

would i have ever been made ready?

there are exactly two ghosts waiting

on coughing heating pipes back home

while dawn wests. we leave the party a stray

bottle rocket. we leave as that which does not want

to leave. we leave as the ghosts we've

gotten so good at becoming. no one is

following us. i know the living fractures thin.

i know you are there, your sliver of death

cloak shadow barely visible. i blow dust

confirming my assertions.

i blow dust to make you visible again

to me. we point at all the little ghosts

around us. they aren't frightening anymore.

they stop bumping in the night.

they start playing cards with us on wednesdays

& dance with us fridays to rnb records.

we begin to prefer them to people.

it all feels quite natural. we eat in

more now too. my apartment is a botanical garden

of chopstick & plastic utensil from

around the world, manufactured in china

& brought to brooklyn, just for us.

& the forest of napkins you call magic

dance over the sea of kitchen linoleum

when the wind moves through them.

we know it's not us nor ghosts, but something

else, bigger than us & ghosts making

our forest dance. & because i know

you're there, they thought i'd become

a priest someday. i could feel the dead

my whole life coming back & staying

dead, a blow of dust, but i want to kiss you,

so don't come back from the dead

merely stardust & atoms. i know how to

conjure up. i know how to dance

to soul records. i know the sound of a radio's

fuzz in nowhere-new mexico where night is

the only thing with arms around us.

& we are older now. we don't have to listen

to people. people have to know

who's closing the doors to the room

they're in, but i don't care. people hide

in plain sight, which we both know is

the most dangerous kind of hidden.

like skylit moon, if it didn't feel so good we wouldn't eat so much of it:

      the sugar, the sex. we wouldn't have

built that storefront for condoms & cashews & hands & legs & lassos

waiting on a credible news source to confirm reports of the recent extinction

      of the unicorn race. a week ago it was reported

the last cowboy died out too. you said you were shocked & entirely skeptical at the same time.

as long as there exists the places we are waiting on

      & the places we will not go,

i am sure unicorns & cowboys are much alive in the fabric of our dna. i whisper into your palm,

      the same palm that reaches & reaches & reaches outward.

you took the news like one takes

      a secret. you thought on it a while. you buried it in the backyard of your head.

you watered it, sang to it before bed & like all things it grew.

just because we can't see cowboys & unicorns

doesn't mean we shouldn't pray

to them, you said, quiet, as to not break the still black morning's sloth.

just because we can't pray to them, doesn't mean there lacks room for us to imagine hooves
against the wooden slats of a saloon, a person riding bareback

with one-handed confidence leading us
from temptation to temptation

& delivering us to a rotunda of night sky, you said.

you wrote a prayer on a notepad:
            unicorn, tell us how all was placed on earth.

you burnt it in a candle. you watched its ashes be carried off to somewhere else. everywhere we exist

is a building waiting for us to
            step out of, & because we grow weary of listening for hooves at night,

in the morning, ivory glistens with dew
            & because children stop dreaming in their beds & later outside of them too, we all must

face our inevitable extinctions. the new others will make tapestries of us then.
            we will not be shown making shapes with arms & legs

nor eating pistachios in bed

but alive again, walking upright. the visitors will say *how happy*
        they look, in the tapestry where we are

chained to a pomegranate tree surrounded by a fence, in a field of eternal celestial bloom

where the flowers know to open for moon, not sun.
        those coming to visit our tapestry will think we didn't know the difference

between our serenity & freedom. *i wonder how they tamed them,*

        the visitors will say. *i wonder if they knew*

they were the last of something? & right now as i think these things in bed,
        on some porch in somewhere-montana a house lamp dims

& the sky a broken yolk above it.

what are you thinking, you say. *no, don't tell me*, you say, waiting for me to
        pull you onto my side of the bed

& the moonlight will make its attempt to pierce
        through the curtains while we both wait.

to what they don't tell you about this line of work

moments when time
is still

& undecided

i consider cb radios

to confirm hypotheses

& the poetry of carrier pigeons, their cooing

so close to coup

i am comforted

by the misinterpretation

of their violence.

the others only see

the edge of this world,

                                                        as a kite

is a decoy

                                                        for a pilot.

people started with hoarding small things: thimbles, thread, antibiotic & syringes. when the news was confirmed, they hoarded larger items: orcas, polar bears, jackals & a yellow school bus. they dug a hole so deep into the earth, oxygen could barely finger it. then the presidents & dictators & celebrities in droves filed into the earth. it was rumored there would be plenty of board games, televisions & visionaries, though pandas weren't invited. neither was alabama, croatia, the sudan, nor chile, among others. i wasn't invited. soon it was just us & the mayans shaking their heads & quiet.

*

as sudden, morning begins

a carnival from the next world over. from the next world over

entertainers is all we are.

as sudden, morning begins

lantern & gaff, flounder gigging
the northern lights

their afterglow wading

into the river to bathe.

someone touches herself.

someone hums.

the world's melting,

only the tinkers

& carnie sideshows could sense it.

they the only ones allowed to leave their kingdoms.

*

i have to remind myself that i asked to live out of a suitcase.
i have to remind myself that i asked for each tomorrow to be new.

in bed, the constant apparition

a moon ebbing from something

into something else.
from the next world over

this world looks like strings of light
attached to two great circles.

as close to what can
touch heaven

as the moths that think they can glow.

people on the television

begin to look more like me.

i make habit of kissing the screen. i consider making

birthday cakes, calling this *the great dance*.

i start using more french in my english. i'm not

lonely because i've renamed
lonely. i've renamed

the world: a puddle
of apricot derision.

i've asked politely, even hoped you'd take your own life before i'd have to.

a drone of violence blossoms this fugue.

i wake up

one morning pleased to meet you.

i take my name the next.

to the tin band that read: keegan matthew lester, 21841 seacrest lane, huntington beach california, eader elementary, the one with a brontosaurus imprint on the top. to the man who told me to believe in what we could not see, & called it science, before telling us they were mistaken. to the letter i received from science a few years back: *we here at science want to apologize. we had our own misgivings, but wanted to see how it would play out. we are sorry about your brontosaurus. there were cartoons & movies & books, we were too late to call it off. museums were doing well. people could look at the scale of our hyperbole for the first time & understand the way we love. we literally made a skeleton of hyperbole, to teach you to dream again. museums kept their lights on, due to things we made up. we got adults to make up stories for children to explain the feasibility of something so large & terrifying & confusing, that only ate plants, that only a comet could have killed. vegetarians loved us in the 90's. now we sell drugs & will be in business for a long time. would you like some drugs? also, pluto: not a planet. sorry about that too. we grew tired of discovering. we wanted to create things, just this one time. we wanted to know what it would feel like to paint rooms for an afternoon. sorry. sincerely, science.* to the prayer science & i wrote together: god rid me of god. god help me give up credibility today, so that i might be able to make something for someone else.

Coda

What I Imagine of the Place You Grew Up In, That You Still Don't Call Home, from Time To Time When Your Voice's Register Catches Me Off Guard & I See You More Than I Hear Your Man Costume

i guess

it's too late

to live out on the farm

to tattoo our eyelids

melt the golden

bars of chain & band

because the floodlight

spoke to me

at the bottom of bayou

last night, where muck

& mud ghost

& cleft lip black snaked

& widowed. i could see the trail

they left before us,

their knees & breasts,

their arms & fingers

dug into that shale sand

& you couldn't tell

just by looking at it

like you can't tell from

a reproduction of a painting,

but the strokes

were all there. i guess

it's too late to live

out on the farm

thrush crushing thrush

with their beaks

beneath that dark blanket of sky

where you said *that noise out there,*

those are angels

killing for other angels because

angels don't kill for god

beneath a blanket of anything

& because i was taught as a boy

that angels do their killing

out in the open

i wear this shirt

for good luck. the doe

sewn inside the cuff

means don't startle so easy,

don't be just a tuft of hair

but, the entire scalp.

be something the others

will have to axe down,

will have to break you from

you, you yourself, from this earth

with silver bullet

with a horse that's not theirs

& thus named in haste

as a name & gravity

are the only way

to get to somewhere else.

You Appalachian Reappropriating Asshole Poets

i don't write about killing deer

because the closest i've ever come to it
is with my car swerving

& i think the rest of you are dishonest. my cousin
dropped a hundred & ten hits of acid

on a road trip to california once. he climbed a foreign mountain

to see the sunrise over a desert foreign to him
along the way. of course he was still on acid

at that point, but also searching

for water. he still sees deer at night
darting from the corner of his eyes

while driving. he does not write poems. he stops

the heartbeat of deer
with his hands & mouth. he cries for his father with his arms

every time i see him. when his father lost the ability to use his hands

& legs, my cousin lined up a rifle
& a deer salt lick, about twenty yards apart.

all his dad would have to do is nudge

the gun from the porch. my great uncle pitched
for the yankees. he also killed deer.

he never wrote a single poem

& i will always love him for it. my cousin wanted

to write a book about his dad. he wanted the first chapter to end

on the day he slipped on a wet step

& broke his neck while golfing, instead, my dad took me hunting once

on the land next to a different uncle's home.

we saw a deer in the meadow.

he took the gun. he aimed it himself.

he missed. it was so goddamn cold that day. a man

came running out shouting *you on tha docta's property, sir.* we scurried

off through the thicket we first entered,

but this time with no caution & i cut up my hands trying

to protect my face. i missed

because i didn't want to deal with cutting up that deer
& cleaning it & dragging it back to jimmy's, my dad said.

this was one of the times i can think of that my dad tried

to protect me from the world. that day we did not
reach into the chest of a life we ended.

we did not have to put anything out of its misery.

nothing ached, but our hands from the cold
& thorns. my cousin wrote

his master's thesis on why people in west virginia are so fat.

he says it's because by-and-large west virginian's don't have enough
money to buy good food. my grandma

had no way of knowing her brother couldn't be a yankee forever. one day

he grabbed a knife the wrong way at a picnic

& he couldn't throw the next. one day

he was either finishing up or about to play a round of golf,

of this fact i've never been sure,

& then he slipped on a wet step.

Ars Poetica

still under construction, the kiss as thunderclouds in summer sky that sometimes means lightning,

as the smell of after-rain. as the dress hanging from anything other than a person: the shadow

it casts, a kind of furrow. as the shape of two people reaching for something far away, reaching

for something like oranges. as miles from home. as the only thing you ever knew about the wild

is that one needed water & a flashlight because reportedly, people get lost in the wild all the time.

as in a hotel room one evening listening to the stranger singing to donavan *yonder stands*

your orphan with his gun, the face joan baez made. as the birds that knew pompeii was blowing,

long before people did & tried to warn people, at a time in history when no one spoke bird.

as the terrible jars of light in our stomachs, there perhaps because of us. as once on your way home

from the party the street back to your house was lined with basketball hoops because a family

on the corner had bought one & before long every house had one & not many of the kids

actually used them & that night the basketball hoops looked especially strange & lonely

guarding the houses, begging to be touched. & you did. as you kissing each & every one

on your way home from the party.

Acknowledgments

poems in this manuscript have previously appeared in the following journals:

The Atlas Review * BackLash Press* Boaat Journal * Boiler Journal * Bort Quarterly * The Boston Review* Conjunctions* Control Literary Magazine * Fissure * FloorPlan * Foundry Journal *Fruita Pulp * The Journal * Map Literary * Reality Beach * Sixth Finch * SINK REVIEW * Sun Dog Lit * Tinderbox * Whiskey Island

Thank you Grandma, for your strength * Thank you to my entire family, you've all supported me in various ways over the years & all contributions have been important * Thank you Isabelle Shepherd for your eyes, ears, brain & heart, for pouring them onto these pages * Thank you Crich for being my secret reader for the last decade, breaker of gates, teacher, friend, & not tiresome. * Thank you Carol, Kathleen & Susan for feeding, housing & being surrogate mothers to me in exchange for poetry, which had no downside for me * Thank you to the entire Tountas / Taylor family for your generosity, love & shelter * Thank you Matthew Revert for being kind, patient, brillant and above all a friend; for being the person I trusted to birth the artifact of this project into the world * Thank you to the entire Slope Editions family * Thank you Mary Ruefle * Thank you to all of my professors at West Virginia University & Columbia University * Thank you Tom Roma for helping me see the magic in poetry, at a time in my life when magic was hard to come by * Thank you Renee for being my literary partner in crime & for your unwavering belief; for pushing me into this Odyssey. * Thank you Mary Ann Samyn for instilling the concrete within me that has served as the foundation of every poem I've written, & for inciting within me the courage to do so * Thank you Scott McClanahan & Eva Maria Saavedra & Tim Donnelly for influencing my writing, your friendship & for allowing me to make you part of this * I was meant for derision / Nothing short of fate itself / Has affected my decision * Thank you Mom, Dad & Paige * I was young when I left home / been rambl'n all around / & I never wrote a letter / to my home. / I don't like it in the wind, / I want to go back home again, / But I can't go home this a'way."

notes on the poems

(to héloïse d'argenteuil & peter abélard.) is for my mother & father

(neither of us can be who we are without football…) the first sentence of this poem comes directly out of the
television program friday night lights —for patty slagel

(deer electric in the air will live another day) for susan, kathleen, & carol

(to all of this which does not just seem, but is extraordinary) for fern, walden, branden and courtney

(dear mother, the first christmas that did not feel like christmas…) for eva

(& these mountains i go to, i go to) for isabelle shepherd

(it begins as it always begins, i couldn't help from thinking) much of this was lifted from friday night lights. for
chris, pat, jimmy & grandpap

(that soon pears would) steals from timothy donnelly both in poem and presence, for mark strand

(1940s berlin in a movie theater, where two strangers touch…) for jack gilbert

(while i was out getting drunk night after night…) for virginia lester

(to the egrets & wasps.) for alyssa and tyler mikev the most beautiful partnership i've ever encountered, thank you
for your friendship

(i thought i saw you again) for paul miller and christo tountas

(like skylit moon, if it didn't feel so good we wouldn't eat so much of it:) for eleni

(to what they don't tell you about this line of work) for judy

(to the tin band that read: keegan matthew lester, 21841…) for huntington beach, ca for tracy, chris & rowan

What I Imagine Of The Place You Grew Up In, That You Still Don't Call Home, From Time To Time When Your
Voice's Register Catches Me Off Guard & I See You More Than I Hear Your Man Costume for scott crichlow

You Appalachian Reappropriating Asshole Poets, for my dad, for morgantown and for west virginia

Ars Poetica for the rices, florida, and my mother for giving me vision